INTRODUCTION

MARIE CURIE, ANNIE OAKLEY, MAYA ANGELOU.

These aren't your grandma's paper dolls! Here, you'll find twenty colorful paper dolls of trailblazing women who changed the world, ready for you to punch out, assemble, and dress for action. Next to each woman, you'll find authentic outfits and accessories that showcase the woman's claim to fame, such as Joni Mitchell's guitar, Joan of Arc's sword, and Frida Kahlo's painting palette.

Each page contains a different activist, scientist, athlete, politician, artist, or entertainer who has broken barriers and reached new heights. Complete with biographies exploring how each woman made her mark and an inspiring quote from the woman herself, this book explores the lives and stories of some of history's greatest movers and shakers.

How do you set up your awesome women paper dolls? First, punch out the paper doll and her accessories from the page. Make your doll stand up by punching out a foot stand from the back of the book, then fitting the center slot of the foot stand into the slot at the bottom of the doll, under her feet, in order to make a cross. Dress your paper doll by laying the outfit or accessory over the doll, and folding the paper tabs over to hold it in place.

Get ready to be inspired as you celebrate the women who put on their flight suits and flying goggles, picked up their pens and picket signs, and got things done.

JOAN OF ARC
b. January 6, 1412 / d. May 30, 1431
CLAIM TO FAME: Led the French army to victory during the Hundred Years' War

Joan of Arc was a peasant woman born in France during the Hundred Years' War with England. During Joan's childhood, France was under English rule, but many French people wished to put the last French king's son, Charles VII, on the throne.

Joan began to have dreams telling her to go to Charles and support him in expelling the English from France. She went in 1429 to offer her help, and her army beat the English back in several battles in May. Joan was only seventeen at the time! Charles was crowned King that July.

Joan led another battle in 1430, where she was injured and captured. Charles chose not to get involved. The English charged Joan with several crimes, primarily heresy, but also witchcraft and dressing like a man. On May 30, 1431, she was burned at the stake at the age of nineteen. Joan of Arc's legacy as a brave and pious fighter continued, and in May 1920, she was canonized as a saint, and she is now the patron saint of France.

SACAGAWEA
b. May 1788 / d. circa 1812
CLAIM TO FAME: Traveled with explorers Lewis and Clark to the Pacific Ocean

Sacagawea was born the daughter of a Shoshone chief in Lemhi Couny, Idaho. She was kidnapped from her village by an enemy tribe around the age of twelve, and sold to a French-Canadian trapper named Toussaint Charbonneau, who took her as a wife.

In November of 1804, Meriwether Lewis and William Clark arrived in present-day North Dakota, where Sacagawea now lived, on their journey to explore new lands and make their way to the West Coast and the Pacific Ocean. Sacagawea and Charbonneau went with them to act as interpreters. Along the journey, Sacagawea helped in many different ways: She translated when they met with Native American tribes, she could identify edible plants, and her presence signaled the group's peaceful intent. She also helped navigate, and in some cases was able to show the men the best places to cross a river or a mountain range. The group reached the Pacific in November 1805.

SUSAN B. ANTHONY
b. February 15, 1820 / d. March 13, 1906
CLAIM TO FAME: Leader in the woman's suffrage movement

Susan B. Anthony was born to a politically active Quaker family, and was introduced to the anti-slavery movement at a young age. She met Elizabeth Cady Stanton at an anti-slavery meeting, and the two soon connected on social issues. Anthony was active with the American Anti-Slavery Society in the years leading up to the Civil War, but soon turned her attentions more directly toward the women's suffrage movement, continuing to work closely with Stanton. The two founded the National Woman Suffrage Association in 1869.

In 1872, Anthony led a group of women to the polls to vote in the presidential election. She was arrested a few days later, and according to some accounts, insisted she be handcuffed, as that's how men were arrested. She was fined $100, but refused to pay. In 1905, she met with President Theodore Roosevelt in support of a proposed amendment that would give women the right to vote. She died in 1906, fourteen years before the 19th Amendment was finally adopted, giving American women the right to vote.

HARRIET TUBMAN
(BORN ARTMINTA ROSS)
b. circa 1822 / d. March 10, 1913
CLAIM TO FAME: Led countless American slaves to freedom

Harriet Tubman was born into slavery on a plantation in Maryland around 1822. In 1849, those who owned her tried to sell her away from her family, and she started planning to escape. She fled with her brothers in September of that year, and Tubman eventually crossed into freedom in Pennsylvania. Over the next eleven years, Tubman took many more expeditions into Maryland, risking her own freedom to lead others to safety: She and her "passengers" on the Underground Railroad were never captured.

Tubman was also active during the American Civil War, when she helped lead a raid on several plantations near the Combahee River, providing the Union with information on the terrain and other intelligence. Later, she participated in the women's suffrage movement alongside Susan B. Anthony. Tubman will grace the new $20 bill, to be released in 2020.

ANNIE OAKLEY
(BORN PHOEBE ANN MOSEY)
b. August 13, 1860 / d. November 3, 1926
CLAIM TO FAME: Leading woman of the American West

Phoebe Ann Mosey was born in a cabin in Ohio, but her rare and "unladylike" skill at shooting brought her before a world audience, entertaining kings, queens, and crowds as part of *Buffalo Bill's Wild West* show. She travelled the world showing off her daring trick shots, including one favorite where she split a playing card, edge-on, in midair. (She probably took the stage name "Oakley" from an area of Cincinnati.) When Oakley met Native American leader Sitting Bull, he nicknamed her "Little Sure Shot."

Oakley was also active in teaching women how to shoot: She is believed to have taught more than 15,000 women the skill across her career. During the Spanish-American War, she wrote to President William McKinley offering the services of herself and 50 "lady sharpshooters," whose services were in turn declined. Oakley's life was later memorialized in a famous Broadway musical, *Annie Get Your Gun*.

MARIE CURIE
(BORN MARIA SALOMEA SKŁODOWSKA)
b. November 7, 1867 / d. July 4, 1934
CLAIM TO FAME: Developed the theory of radioactivity; won two Nobel Prizes

Although she was a bright student, Curie could not attend the men-only University of Warsaw, so she took classes in secret instead. She later traveled to Paris to study, and there she met and married Pierre Curie. In 1898, the Curies announced their discovery of the elements polonium and later radium.

In 1903, the Curies and their research partner Henri Becquerel received the Nobel Prize in physics for their study of radioactivity. Marie was the first woman to receive that prize. When Pierre died in 1906, Marie was given his position as a professor at the University of Paris—the first woman to hold the position at that university. Curie won a second Nobel Prize in 1911, this time in chemistry.

Curie died in 1934 from her longtime exposure to radiation. Her notebooks and writings are kept in a lead-lined box at the French Bibliothèque Nationale—but people who read them need to wear protective clothing, since they are still dangerously radioactive!

ELEANOR ROOSEVELT
(BORN ANNA ELEANOR ROOSEVELT)
b. October 11, 1884 / d. November 7, 1962
CLAIM TO FAME: The first politically active U.S. First Lady; later a member of the United Nations

Eleanor Roosevelt was born in New York City in 1884 to well-off and politically connected family; she was the niece of President Theodore Roosevelt. At age twenty-one, she married Franklin D. Roosevelt, who was a distant cousin.

Franklin became president in 1933, and due to her own passionate personality and her husband's polio, Roosevelt took on a more prominent political role than previous First Ladies. She gave speeches and press conferences about women's and children's issues and human rights, wrote a newspaper column titled "My Day," and settled a dispute with a group of WWI veterans. She also openly supported the civil rights movement, and invited many black guests to the White House.

After her husband's death in 1945, she served as the chair of the United Nations Commission on Human Rights. There, she helped draft the Universal Declaration of Human Rights, which she considered her greatest accomplishment. Roosevelt later served again in the UN, when President John F. Kennedy assigned her to chair the President's Commission on the Status of Women.

AMELIA EARHART
b. July 24, 1897 / d. (disappeared) July 2, 1937
CLAIM TO FAME: First female aviator to fly across the Atlantic and Pacific Oceans

Amelia Mary Earhart was born in Atchison, Kansas in 1897, but moved around quite a bit during her childhood. Earhart became interested in flying after standing her ground when an airshow pilot "buzzed" by her while she watched the show. In 1923, she became the sixteenth woman to be issued a pilot's license. In addition to her flight across the Atlantic Ocean, Earhart also was the first woman to fly across North America solo, flew in a number of air races, and set a world altitude record (of 18,415 feet) in 1931. Earhart encouraged other women to take up the activity; she was heavily involved with The Ninety-Nines, an international organization of women pilots, of which she became the first president in 1930.

In 1937, she attempted a flight around the world. While hers was not the first round-the-world flight, it would have been the longest because she was following a route close to the equator. Earhart disappeared on July 2, just short of finishing her voyage.

FRIDA KAHLO
(BORN MAGDALENA CARMEN FRIEDA KAHLO Y CALDERÓN)
b. July 6, 1907 / d. July 13, 1954
CLAIM TO FAME: Beloved Mexican painter and feminist icon

Frida Kahlo was a Mexican artist famed for her beautiful paintings, specifically her self-portraits. At age nineteen, she was seriously injured in a bus accident; she was bedridden, and turned her focus to painting. Her art style has been called surrealist, and takes inspiration from traditional Mexican art, using bold colors and traditional symbols, such as monkeys. Her work is also sometimes considered Mexican folk art, and has strong feminist overtones.

Throughout her career, Kahlo painted many famous works, including *The Suicide of Dorothy Hale* (1939), *The Two Fridas* (1939), and *The Broken Column* (1944). Her painting *The Frame* was purchased to be displayed in the Louvre. Her most famous works were her self-portraits, which were deeply personal and illustrated her perspective of life events, including her relationship with her husband, the famous Mexican muralist Diego Rivera, and her struggles with her health.

LUCILLE BALL
b. August 6, 1911 / d. April 26, 1989
CLAIM TO FAME: Groundbreaking comedian who ran her own television production studio

Lucille Ball started her career as a model, and worked her way up in commercials, as an extra, and in several B-movies. She met Cuban bandleader Desi Arnaz in one of her films, and the two married in 1940. Arnaz encouraged Ball to try television, and *I Love Lucy* hit the small screen in 1951. The couple was able to negotiate full ownership rights to the show, and produced it themselves under their company, Desilu Productions. *Lucy* became the top show in the country, and Ball became a star.

After the show ended in 1957, Desilu Productions continued to create hit shows like *Mission: Impossible* and *Star Trek*. She and Arnaz divorced in 1960, and Ball bought out the remainder of Desilu, making her the first woman to own a production company. Ball continued to be widely recognized as a groundbreaking comedian and actress, and received many awards for her work, including four Primetime Emmys, the Lifetime Achievement Award from the Kennedy Center Honors, and two stars on the Hollywood Walk of Fame.

QUEEN ELIZABETH II
(BORN ELIZABETH ALEXANDRA MARY OF THE HOUSE OF WINDSOR)
b. April 21, 1926
CLAIM TO FAME: Longest-reigning monarch in British history

Elizabeth Alexandra Mary was born in 1926. Her father was crowned King George VI in 1936, after his brother abdicated the throne. During World War II, when she was only fourteen, Elizabeth gave a calm and levelheaded radio address to comfort the children of England. When she was older, she briefly served on the Auxiliary Territorial Service as a driver and mechanic. She fell in love with Philip Mountbatten; they married in 1947, and her first son, Charles, was born in 1948. After her father's death, she was crowned queen in June 1953, and the ceremony was broadcast on TV for the first time in history.

Queen Elizabeth continues to serve her people, although her son Prince Charles has taken on some of her responsibilities. She enjoys the company of her family, including her young great-grandchildren, as well as her much-beloved corgis.

MAYA ANGELOU
(BORN MARGUERITE ANNIE JOHNSON)
b. April 4, 1928 / d. May 28, 2014
CLAIM TO FAME: Poet and author; civil rights activist

Maya Angelou was raised in the South in the 1930s and '40s. She had a son at 16. In 1953, she married Anastasios Angelopulos, from whom she took her professional name.

In the 1950s and '60s, Angelou performed in plays and musicals, recorded calypso music, and travelled extensively. Upon returning to the U.S., she moved to New York and began to focus on her writing, joining the Harlem Writers Guild. She met many black writers and activists, including Martin Luther King Jr. In the mid-1960s, she worked with Malcolm X in the civil rights movement.

In 1969, she published her memoir *I Know Why the Caged Bird Sings*, which became a bestseller. It was also the first nonfiction work by an African-American woman to achieve that level of success. Angelou went on to write books, music, screenplays, and other creative works, including a collection of poetry titled *Just Give Me a Cool Drink of Water 'fore I Diiie*, which won the Pulitzer Prize.

RUTH BADER GINSBURG
(BORN RUTH JOAN BADER)
b. March 15, 1933
CLAIM TO FAME: Second female justice appointed to the Supreme Court; advocate of civil and women's rights

Ruth Joan Bader was born in Brooklyn. She attended Cornell, graduating first in her class in 1954. Ginsburg enrolled at Harvard in 1956, and she soon became the first female member of the *Harvard Law Review*. She taught law for several years at Rutgers and then Columbia, where she was the school's first tenured female professor.

Ginsburg consistently advocated for women in her law work, cofounding the Women's Rights Project at the ACLU in 1972, the year before she became the General Counsel for the organization. She took on many cases as chief litigator for her Women's Rights Project, including *Duren v. Missouri*, which made women's service on a jury required, as it was for men (it had previously been optional).

In 1980, President Carter appointed her to the U.S. Court of Appeals, and then in 1993, President Clinton appointed her to the Supreme Court. She has served the court for more than twenty years.

JANE GOODALL
(BORN VALERIE JANE MORRIS-GOODALL)
b. April 3, 1934
CLAIM TO FAME: Foremost expert on chimpanzees; conservationist

Valerie Jane Morris-Goodall first visited Africa in 1957, where she met paleontologist Louis Leakey, who asked her to work with him to study primates. In July 1960, Goodall travelled to the Gombe Stream National Park in Tanzania and began studying the chimps that lived there. She observed that chimps use tools to "fish" for ants in anthills, and that they hunt and eat small mammals—previously people thought chimps were vegetarian. Goodall also named the chimps she observed (instead of numbering them), and noticed that the chimps displayed unique personalities, a new idea at the time.

She also noticed what humans were doing to the land near her research center in Africa, and began speaking out about conservation. She founded the Jane Goodall Institute in 1977 to protect chimps' habitats and the communities around them. Goodall was honored as a United Nations Messenger of Peace in 2002 for her work.

JONI MITCHELL
(BORN ROBERTA JOAN ANDERSON)
b. November 7, 1943

CLAIM TO FAME: Influential singer and songwriter of iconic pop and folk songs of the 1960s and 1970s; often considered the "voice of a generation"

Roberta Joan Anderson was an athletic child, but was weakened by polio at the age of nine, and turned her attention toward music. She taught herself to play the guitar and sang at parties, and later at small local venues. Joni became pregnant in 1964, but gave the child up for adoption, a painful experience that was reflected in her music. (She was reunited with her daughter in 1997.)

Her lyrics and music attracted attention, and in 1968, she recorded *Song to a Seagull*, her first album. She continued putting out popular albums, winning a Grammy for Best Folk Performance in 1969 for *Clouds*, then releasing *Ladies of the Canyon*, which included classics like "Big Yellow Taxi." She experimented with jazz in later albums, winning another Grammy for *Court and Spark*. She has released more than twenty-five albums, including *Blue* in 1971, *Both Sides Now* in 2000, and *Songs of a Prairie Girl* in 2005. In 1997, she was inducted into the Rock and Roll Hall of Fame, and into the Canadian Songwriter's Hall of Fame in 2007.

BILLIE JEAN KING
(BORN BILLIE JEAN MOFFITT)
b. November 22, 1943

CLAIM TO FAME: Former World #1 tennis player; advocate of gender equality; one of the first openly gay professional sports figures

Billie Jean King was raised in an athletic family and participated in sports at a young age. She turned heads in 1961 when she and Karen Hantze Susman won the women's doubles title in Wimbledon. King spoke about the need to welcome more women into tennis as she continued to win. She created the Women's Tennis Association in 1973. That same year, she threatened to boycott the U.S. Open if they did not make the cash prizes equal for male and female players.

In 1973, tennis star Bobby Riggs challenged King to a match, popularly called the "Battle of the Sexes." King won. King went on winning, with 39 major singles, doubles, and mixed-doubles championships. King was outed as gay by a lawsuit from a former lover in 1981, and the fallout rocked her career. She was dropped from many endorsements, but became an icon in the gay community. She was inducted into the International Tennis Hall of Fame in 1987.

HILLARY CLINTON
(BORN HILLARY DIANE RODHAM)
b. October 26, 1947

CLAIM TO FAME: Former U.S. Senator and Secretary of State; first female presidential nominee from a major party

Hillary Rodham Clinton was inspired to public service from a young age after hearing Martin Luther King Jr. speak in her hometown of Chicago. She attended Yale Law School, where she met Bill Clinton. They married in 1975, and their daughter Chelsea was born in 1980. Bill was elected president in 1993, and served two terms. Hillary was an active First Lady and worked alongside her husband to support healthcare reform and women's rights. Hillary ran for office after leaving the White House, winning the New York U.S. Senator seat in 2000.

In 2007, she announced her decision to run for president, but was beaten in the primaries by Barack Obama. Obama appointed her to his cabinet as his Secretary of State. In 2015, Clinton announced her intention to run again for president. This time, she was chosen as the candidate for the Democratic party. Her campaign focused on education, the environment, and social justice.

SALLY RIDE
b. May 26, 1951 / d. July 23, 2012

CLAIM TO FAME: First American woman in space

Sally Ride was raised in California and graduated from Stanford with a bachelor's degree in English and physics and later a master's and PhD in physics. She joined NASA in 1978.

Ride travelled into orbit with the crew of the *Challenger* in 1983 and again in 1984. Prior to her missions, Ride parried media questions such as "Do you weep when things go wrong on the job?" with, "How come nobody asks Rick those questions?," presumably referring to Captain Rick Hauck, pilot of the mission. After Ride left NASA in 1987, she worked as a professor of physics at the University of California, San Diego; as director of the California Space Institute; and manager of several NASA outreach programs.

Sally Ride died in 2012 of pancreatic cancer. Her obituary revealed her twenty-seven-year relationship with fellow scientist and professor Tam O'Shaughnessy, who now manages the Sally Ride Science company, which creates science programming for kids, particularly young women.

OPRAH WINFREY
b. January 29, 1954

CLAIM TO FAME: Award-winning talk show host, actress, television producer, and notable trendsetter

Oprah Winfrey is a cultural icon, and a media mogul, who has worked her way into a prominent place in the American culture, in print, on television, and behind the scenes.

Winfrey got her start in 1976, hosting the talk show *People Are Talking* in Baltimore for a very successful eight years. In 1983, a Chicago TV station asked her to host a morning show, *A.M. Chicago*, competing against the likes of Phil Donahue. The show was a takeoff success, and brought Oprah forcefully into the public eye.

Oprah then appeared in the Spielberg film *The Color Purple* in 1985, and was nominated for an Oscar. She began *The Oprah Winfrey Show* in 1986: nationally syndicated, with a peak audience of 10 million viewers. Oprah secured the ownership of the show from ABC, under her Harpo Productions company. It had a strong focus on self-help, health, and self-empowerment.

In 1996, she created the Oprah Book Club, and in 2000, she cofounded the Oxygen Media television network to produce programs for women. Her magazine, *O, The Oprah Magazine*, has been published monthly since April 2000. Winfrey ended her show in 2011 and turned her attentions toward her Oprah Winfrey Network.

Oprah has used her clout to support causes such as children's rights and girls' educations in Africa, and uses a great portion of her immense wealth to support a variety of charities.

MISTY COPELAND
b. September 10, 1982

CLAIM TO FAME: First African-American woman principal ballerina at the American Ballet Theater

Misty Copeland didn't start practicing ballet until age thirteen—most ballerinas start much younger—but by the age of fifteen, she was honored with the Los Angeles Music Center Spotlight Award. The *Los Angeles Times* called her the best young dancer in the area. Copeland joined the prestigious American Ballet Theater in 2000 and became a soloist in 2007, continuing until 2015. She danced in productions such as *Firebird*, *Sleeping Beauty*, and *Swan Lake*, with her grace and skill praised by audiences and critics.

In 2015, she was promoted to principal ballerina, the highest rank in the dance company. Copeland continues to dance with the ABT. She has also appeared in a music video with Prince and on the television show *So You Think You Can Dance*, and has published a children's book titled *Firebird*, which has an inspirational message for children of color.

JOAN OF ARC

"One life is all we have and we live it as we believe in living it. But to sacrifice what you are and to live without belief, that is a fate more terrible than dying."

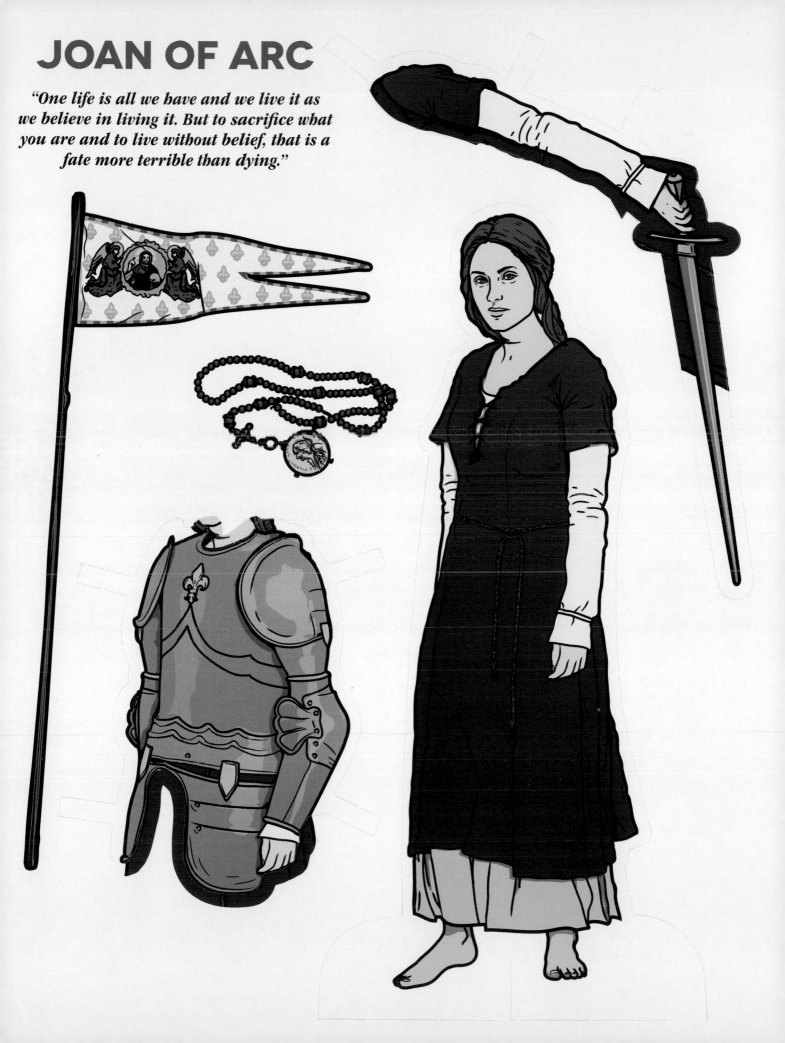

SACAGAWEA

"Everything I do is for my people."

HARRIET TUBMAN

"I can't die but once."

ANNIE OAKLEY

"Aim at a high mark and you will hit it."

MARIE CURIE

"I am among those who think that science has great beauty."

ELEANOR ROOSEVELT

"It isn't enough to talk about peace. One must believe in it. And it isn't enough to believe in it. One must work at it."

AMELIA EARHART

"I want to do it because I want to do it. Women must try to do things as men have tried. When they fail, their failure must be but a challenge to others."

FRIDA KAHLO

"They thought I was a Surrealist, but I wasn't. I never painted dreams. I painted my own reality."

LUCILLE BALL

"I'm not funny. What I am is brave."

QUEEN ELIZABETH II

"The true measure of all our actions is how long the good in them lasts . . . everything we do, we do for the young."

MAYA ANGELOU

"You can't use up creativity. The more you use, the more you have."

RUTH BADER GINSBURG

"If you're going to change things, you have to be with the people who hold the levers."

JANE GOODALL

"Only if we understand can we care. Only if we care will we help. Only if we help shall they be saved."

JONI MITCHELL

"When the world becomes a massive mess with nobody at the helm, it's time for artists to make their mark."

BILLIE JEAN KING

"Champions keep playing until they get it right."

HILLARY CLINTON

"If there is one message that echoes forth from this conference, let it be that human rights are women's rights and women's rights are human rights once and for all."

SALLY RIDE

*"When you're getting ready to launch into space,
you're sitting on a big explosion waiting to happen."*

OPRAH WINFREY

"You are your possibilities. If you know that, you can do anything."

MISTY COPELAND

"The path to your success is not as fixed and inflexible as you think."